Dedicated

to Emma Davie and Derek LeBlanc

for teaching, despite being teachers.

D1580624

TO
ERIN
KEEP ON POOPING
and look after
your thumb X

The biggest of mistakes can be forgiven
But a snowball of little white lies will crush your house.

Guy Garvey

Contents

Contents

Aspinal Street

There you are at the living room ink stained table
Not so frantic
Your eye unmoving from the corner of the room
You're shaking
From the corner of the room
The Light
So faint
Under the wood of floor
The rooms so empty
You're so full
No colour of childish toys
Not yet
What are you doing on that wine stained table
What is that in your hands?
The whole world
The whole room
Wants to see
I do
Just a crack in your fingers
Please ?
Why must we narrators
Be chained so ?

I must know
Is it cocodamol ?
The Light Grows
Flickering unlike your gaze
You are tasked
I must see

"It's just plasticine .
Blue
Unlike fire
I'm building
I'm working on a safe little clever little hand
Delicately delicately
The fingers so fragile
My fingers so fraught
It must be perfect
Or it must be nought
That hand needs a sleeve
To be fed
Cherished
And given strawberries and lime"

It's growing
It's growing
It lights me

It will not even fade her colour

With its glow

Not even an unshaping

Tiny hand

Little neat nails

A body, no breasts

A navel

Perfect

The eyes took 6 years of my care

My attention it shows

They shine so, a challenge to the not so little fire but always I

keep them covered

The tiny shoes

Tiny little blue laces

Masterpieces

Pretend adult jeans

The little wrinkles like trees knots

At each join

What an expression

Like real life won't touch her

Like there's no such thing as cancer to her

Like she's already in on the joke

The puffs of sock at the almost bottom

So believable with a freckle right in the middle to render the

whole thing inconceivable

The wrinkle in her nose took years and a mirror
Are those eyes ever sleeping?
What colour.
What fucking colour

The Fire

"Like fire does all at once, it burns like dominoes like bombs like
balloons and like conversations through the fabric on my back
with its serrated tongues it's tendril teeth it grows despite me like
trees I've enveloped her like water
Clutching holding hugging like a stomach.
It eats at the foundation, the film of my skin the cushion of my
spine, then mesh, then bone, then deep bone, marrow I'd scream
in agony but my lips are at her ears then it heats the blood,
blisters the nerves, burns the heart right through from the other
side of all of me
But
It never
Never
It never
Touches Mollie ."

Kurt Spurt

Do you know what you did to us?
As you almost died
How dare you make it so you can't swallow
Have you no respect?
The propping open
Of your semi jammed windows
That's my fault
You jump from your eyes
You full yourself
More fool us
Don't you know what poison does?
Only the the empty fill themselves
My scars are separate
My cuttings are different
Tiger
Translations
Of fear;
Anger

I want to wrap you
But I'll choke you
I am the mother of you child my child is the mother of me

Just stop eating glass babe
Just stop eating glass
Walk out into the encompassing
Trailing lines of whispers and smoke

Look at those tiny clever hands
You did that
Look at the marks on your hieroglyphic fingers
You did
The blanket forts are claustrophobic
When you're tall
Take off my lips and place them on the table
Because a problem shared is a problem doubled
I'm sorry
I'm so sorry
But have you people ever thought
Of the heavy stones you make me swallow in utter silence
Without utterance
They don't just gather in my stomach
They feel different in different parts
Tight under ribs
Bloated beneath
The weight from the shoulders
And would drown from the feet up

When you're behind the back of one
You're looking in the eyes of one

Please don't turn me to wall
Please keep reading my books
I just want to fill you so full
There's no more room left

For the cocodamol

The cool blood in the grass still rests over the tops of the feet
But it is darlings draining I assure you
Flickering back all around us the distinguishable shapes of
people and trees
O' beauty my trembling gift
The coldness got in
But not under
Foetal
Surround me so round in your edges
Fill up the around me
With space for comfortable breath
The draw
The deliver
You lift me
From
The seat of my knees
So long
As flat as my feet
The same thing
As if the throwing of our tears
Was
Conversations

Agonised beauty I thought I'd lost you
But your cries were enough to elevate me from the all
encompassing
"Mum, y"
The same thing
Almost

Otherwise
it's like talking in shout and never
talking
I'm walking so faintly
The place tilted toward the sky
The base coat bright
I am made of dots
All is made of dots
And lines,
and lines
The loudness does stop
Love does halt it's screech
Oh how the ugly blandness of seeds do hold so secret the
universes.
Oh how how weary the wasps do waiver
I am yearnless
I am selfless
I am I am I am

It must be dark and sticky
Sometimes
On my bloated belly

I lunge each letter
At the yang
In the unpoetic poetic upset
I rhyme
This constant spin
Is
The fun.
None scream ecstasy
Standing still
There is no

composers birthed by comfort.

Alexandra Yearn

There the grass on our feet
Traffic encircling in its consistent circles
The lights that spin us
Never did touch us
The empty of space
Your body bent by your tears you call mine
Still our shudders are harmonic
Still music
I'm pulling on all the stings together and forming what looks
kind of human
Both my best friends are dying from the same barrages of glass
bullets
I am the glass blower of best friends for others
Sometimes I make the shot too

You slunch yourself to the bottom of a tree in the broken grass
leaves
You feel affinity
You blame me
Our eyes are now the level of children
obsession with lights that run circles
The glare of constant

under stars of surely mere moments

We drip tear

Fear the drown

While breathing soundly

Neath the ocean of unknown

You ask if forever is never

Am

I on a

Train to Lincoln ?

Bethany Seed

Love like colours bursting fourth from dark green
indistinguishable, unmanageable forever tied bound and fenced
forever mixing beauty with blank weeds

Friendship lands, it can leave, dancing yellow in open open
ocean blue like warm bees if it's to kiss my petals again it's
because it chose to be here walking with me

Sean Discon

Perfect climate, man made temperatures it's in greenhouses we now grow love.

Where once wild almost empty fields birthed flowers in soil of chance and through the trials of great skies above.

Can we really find it here?

With databases and statistics and brown eyes replaced by pixels on screens?

Without the graze of nervous fingers almost held, listening to the fears of someone else,

In this fake much safer somewhere else there is but one solace to me

chaos.

I'm control

I am control

I'll make you shudder, I'll stop your breath, it's mine, beg me to breathe, your muscles are my muscles, I've them trapped, tense, not tease, locked,

pent. Pent.

I could realise you

I don't

Beg me to let you

It's like pain on your face paint crack

An over bearing

It almost hurts, almost

A little death

bed

Under you

Not enough breath left in

So much fucking inflating

Fucking

I can stop

I could

I do

Hold your breath
I am your throat
Your eyes I close them
Your ears are filled with my air
All of the inches of your nerves I've froze them.
They burn
I could take your hand and move you
I could take your heart and stop it.
Little death.

All that you have left is your voice
Use it
Cum.

Isabel Thrump

Heads under earth
Buried, inhume
Where do they come from ?
The one before it ?
Or
The one before it ?
The one before that
Or the one after ?
The skin will crack and realise it's dead hair
Is the Godot the farmer ?
He who plucks ?
Or
he who plants.

Don Bloom

My best friend
Went into the wrong classroom
And decided to kill himself
And he would of done it too,
I'm going to miss him .

Hanson Yint

Last night I voided in a tea cup
Genuinely
Please don't read that as a metaphor
I'm not being clever
I didn't invent this
This is poetic yet still true
Completely
I pissed in a tea cup.
A teacup filled with
Sterile hot water,
Human Blood
Toilet roll,
There were no tissues
At my friends house or my couchhome
And I think in there I accidentally lost a sharpener
I'm part of her
An accidental sharpener deconstructed
Taken apart on purpose

And I write this
In the poshest of toilets
I sought it out

I needed another piss.

Alana Orchard

I have found a value in eyes
Ted's eyes
I have seen your obsessions
I saw the scrutiny in blue
Overlay
The Alan in your Key
Like Descartes you have disguise
My tiny deaths will forever
Haunt you
But
No longer haunt you as only Carol
But as Sylvie
For in every second line
I will keep my children, my darlings
Outside.

Evyln Sandas

The silver is dull and metal,
man made
With my finger I hold it on outstretched limb
A pinch
The thumb I roll
up and down
back and forth
Depression and euphoria
I'm lying on my arm
Moving nothing it feels poetic
to stop everything to stop blinking
But my thumb and forefinger
Up
Down.
Up
Down.
Then there's a subtle position where the dull sliver holds
the sun.

Fuck myself away from you
Thrust in the oppositey direction
Use this sex as therapy or as a vehicle, use it
But do not use the recipient
Swim a stroke in another lane
The big bowl a pool with pussy juice. Fuck it what am I to you
Go fuck your own on big big boy
Can I ever truly love without the effect of you ?
Not despite you
Not to find you
Can I ever truly live without the repress that's you ?
I can't ever not love you
I want others, to experience life and love through a kaleidoscope
of constantly altering shapes and colours of bodies
And when I'm pushing my hot line of lust into another they are
the only true colour
I'm going to open a hole where there isn't one, in my skin
Let the blood push out all of my personal in.
Wrap a rope around myself and give up my temporal life to a
constant gravity.
I'm going to find the unswallowable
Something too big to fit the whole thing in at once, pull the skin
between my jaw around it and swallow

Or be simplistic and stop eating, writing or breathing
Until life leaves
Take a knife that's long enough to make me insecure long enough
to find an important vain
Give up the endless act
Drop the straining muscle that holds up the lie and be swallowed
by truth
And make the world wet
Like your unfaithless fanny

I'm going to take back control no more influence
Let you forever murder me.

Sebastien Runch

In fear and trembling
Of the utterly usual
Hold the blanket I call bed over the chemical I call head
Through fibrous cracks
I can see the rested white
Filter and fumble through to unrested blue.

Grotesque line drawings
In a crude shaking hand
O' wire frames in thread
O' poetry in inaccessible head

Reality like lucid photography
A hobby
A subjective universal
Like crushed sticky ice
Like bubble bath between body
The descended white
Fleckturiuos paint
A guttural mumble
Murmur of mashing nausea in the crowd.
The film over the fake wood

Water on the tongue
Thought lack food.
Only children can't sleep
These water logged paper blue boundaries
This kindling soaked kerosene
Steel iodine on woollen ball
open
weave
Freeverse ruleless conformity
The urge to eat
The lack of piss and sleep
Fragility
All the lines hung sodden from a mop
All the life on planet Earth
Constantly incidental
Chronically monumental
Like long lifted drunk talk
The mud walls around puddle holes
Like the desperate handfuls of semen sleeping pills.
All I have is poetry
This is why it's a danger to be unperceived by love too long

I am all alone in the inevitable flickering, in the dimming the
translucent sound in the cascading reactory effecting me nowly
but arcing far in history

A lonesome dadless playground prisoned child thing isolated by the very idea of ideas, all real people lost, fictional or musically unattainable
Like the human heart
Or the father ours

I pushed so so sogentle
gainst the skin of the wetbread world
I made a handwritten hole
And watched all that deep damp
Deep damp blood.
Trickle.
Flow.

Deirdre Forest

No one ever doubted us
No one ever doubted them
Some doubted me
Some doubted you
The irony of all this is you're scared of me or my potential.
We can build a house
We should be careful of the carpet
The breathless frantic death of two children
One slightly younger than the other
Of two woman
One slightly saner than the other
The same gas we disbursed
Into the same lovers universe
The same Crow to visit me alone
Duct tape the length of a door
The same reason
The same
Stick thin
Cut skin
Steadily flaking
Steadfast
Wise Woman

In a bell jar
Like them, we are love.
Foxes and flora.

I'm going to start on the back, slow suggestions of fingers tracing the outline of your spine, the occasional nail, charged with tingle, your blood will slow, your breaths level, you will be calm after hours. Let me lie here and watch your breaths move your back, in and out, in and in and out. Then when your calm again... Calm after the days of not, I will move too far down, far too far down my hands push your hips down and you move like butter. Force and firmness. Your mine, I will turn you.

You've been calm but now it breaks like swollen silence. Like surfaces of lakes only wetter.

My hands on your hips pulling at them pulling them apart, I will kiss you hard, mouth, neck shoulderstomach, the tongue a tease

And I will stop right there and wait your begging to go on.
I wait until you beg me.

I move down,

       down,

              down... My fingers twist at your silk, strings tighten like instruments between my fingers, but it's my teeth that

pull them from you, I rip them off like a hunger like impulse I
want to eat you to gorge myself on that pussy but I don't
 I compose myself

You

Are

So
Wet

Is that for me ? Is that all for me?

I'm in charge.

Slowly so slowly

I tease your soft flesh open with my tongue, I taste you, that taste.
That taste. Like sustenance. Like salted caramel but flesh, moist
like sirloin or fillet steak and so fucking warm.

That warmth

Pulsing,
pushing

I want you so hard.

But I'm thrusting my tongue into you now flicking at you like a light switch, making you fill your lungs and my mouth with your warmth.

You fill

You fill me

I will fuck you.

Mrs Crosby.

Ludovico Slome

Passagiggo.
Memories made of music.
I recall the tracing so gentle
Like the teeth are instead soft baby surface
He plays it too fast.
How you could be so timid so reserved
true beauty then
Our foundations arose around me
Up from the stinking earth of squallier and pizza cardboard and
cum then came

Four walls one of which featured paint
The carpet, a carpet bare feet could trust sole gainst truest the
nylon soft sand like the mornings of holidays and glimmers of
families.
The only thing allowed to engulf me, our flowers and odd things
picked to fill spaces between but they needn't be, like the piano
white on black of stars and night cars role reversals and
why now.
That note.
The repeat
But this space didn't need filled

we could put our children inside but we aren't forced its like the
silence after orgasm or before a kiss
It just is

But now the wall on the top left
Is red
And unbeautifal
Human
All clothings fall folded flaccid
It bares all
And you can't bare it
The nooks, the nails
The softest of fingers
Grace the notes from these walls
We can be naked now
Never nude.

Jane Mudd

Speak in only blood braille
Please don't take my motivation from me, please
I need that to breathe.
This is all pretend cardboard to the ones I trust for genuinity
I feel then think
Like the pain then the trip to grazed knee.
A way of consuming reality
I can't see.
I wish this all didn't rhyme.
There's nothing grand about us.

It's like standing on two extremes of pyramidal space, concave,
convex,   everything.

There's no reason for this that's the reason

There's no reason for it, I'm smarter than that, it just is, like the
entire human universe but it hurts when it fills me I've had my fill
of concrete

How can we
How can we
Be happy in a world in which being upset is a cliché

Aesop Blothe

Every hour, monitor moods
hook me up to the fucking factory
That's the factory of fuckers
Not the funny fucking expletive.
Do you even know how you feel? What even is a feeling anyway ?
Even
anyway, what is feeling in any way.
Just water ball.
My bubbles burn pop, skull just a soap filled prism.
the only thing I could have possibly used to diagnose this schism,
still I think we agree a far more honest diagnosis than skin
covered chemistry.
rise and fall in the contradictory

A couple flow charts or a couple couples to study the flow
I am more lonely than the patchwork-boxheads will ever know
And I'll never, no.

Feather fissured Ferris metal
migrate and magnate without any certainty.
This is not a rap not even poetry
Not even poetry

Change

Compartmentalise

Another word an iPhone won't recognise because they can't feel
not like me.

I'm so alone in my subjectivity

Wonky John Paul what have you done to me?

If you know him like I do you'll see the irony

it's satire, on my hat

Almost my hour done

Base our entire understanding of all things we are ever have been
or ever could become on the weather filed bubble birds.

Samuel Gorn

I'm not walking right
My kitten kissed shoulders are all squashed
upLaurenceOlivierLyndons shrug; why can't I cut myself right
We can't we cut ourselves right
Statuesque.
Stone has substance, foundation
I'm more like air
Not wind, directionless
think trapped or claustrophobic
Not air
Water salted water, unnatural water eking from orifices
disgusting thick water
No freshness
Compacted water
Stuck like speechless stone
And untouchable like breathless
Air
Even breath has direction
Maybe the void
There's no comparison
There's nothing .

Cathy Prim

Step over it like a corpse in the road
Why can't I except you to be exceptional ?
You're supposed to have hidden super powers like my mum
Fuck you for having your own pent problems
Replacement is the biggest word I know.
I never once said I didn't want you there.

Roger Moore

I know you see but do you look
You must glance the faces?   Forever empty chair.
The time now
The date soon
And we are all the pebbles rounded separate by the same sea .
Do you know what it all means?
It isn't Thursday
It's my birthday.   I am reading Sartre
Gaze reflective into semi developed memories, like a frozen flat
versions of a me or dead leaves.
I see the faces.

To age, have successful sex and meet you.
To see your face,
inside his face,
like my face and
face it
As you never would
My child will not learn how to cry like I do

A pile of paint equal to the weight of a paintbrush
Lift the heavy from my eyes
Casual the creases
She's like a little volume
I genuinely feel different now I've read subjective words that died
at her hand and rebirthed at my head.
Reality is but a, so is it her fault I'm in love
Her doing
Her choice
Responsibility
Reflected feelings,
Feelings too?
I don't have to try but I do
Surely one is in love
Surely one is in love and one in love with being loved.
Is that a fallacy?
A fallacy on which to build family.
The artist and the muse.
Two muses breed no paint.
Two artists never truly look.

Charlotte Hade

Pull my surfaceskin in two directions imagine the sound as it
rips, out pulses the blue paint to coat myself in so me is me I is I
again it's been so long.
All the wet sex and dry kiss happens outside of my eyes
Everything can be separated from mind, privy to my earthy
organs but not the several universes inside.
Why can't you cheat on me again?
Now I find that knife has been sharpened on both sides.
Every night I grow a new me for you to love, or not,
your
choice

Douglas Gunch

Why do fingers fold in three places?
The first for fists
The second grip
But three ?
Sex needs none but
straightened like cocks
Building needs two like a fight
Why three ?
Why can we keep one, two, all but three straight?
Surely, no
Surely only to
Starve the shared air
Surely only to stop the talk
to strangle,
Surely only a neck slots there
Thumb applies pressure
You have the power to make me gag
Surely only my neck fits
Fragile, breakable, control, pipeline of the only hole a
neck.neck.neck.neck neck.neck.
With these hands only can I envision you dad, so tall.
Your third fold purpose is, in childish memory, no mystery at all.

You were supposed to keep me safe.

Anita Arorus

The full envelopment by you
The dirt and fucking muck on the knees, a skin of blood
Something lost from me
Something gained in you
They call it waves
The electric water that teases at the nooks and the gaps in your
spines, bones
Grass growing at full speed, more
All things evolving
Growing
Pulsing
Wetness
Warmth

...

Darcey Pathos

You filler of every hole
With any cock or voice that fits
There is more to hearts than fucks
Seconds of a lack of a voice
All your pretence of love
I'm sorry my family isn't good enough
How dare you pretend to care without knowing you don't and
never have
The silence that screams hadn't even drawn mighty breath
You are a liar who doesn't know your mind. Like us all
But
I didn't answer one question
And you bout turn
Ask another
Another
Another
What am I to you?
Do I even have a face?
Name one lover or sad poet who show ed me the intake the
output of breath.
Who is Walt Whitman
Or am I an arm, the walk home a voice a little better than your

own the disregarded cum of someone.

To give cum as someone

To theone.

Not someone.

i am so scared especially of men

Every painting shudders
To big to frame
These aren't photos
I don't remember much
I remember
The ruffness of your fingers gagging, a fear of gagging
Every detail of your belt
The gold eagle, the stem of metal, the ball how it pushed against
the hole in the dead skin dark leather, your grip, the static sound
of your beard, the hardness of the hair, the highs, the lows of
your voice, murmurs, what your pants looked like, blue boxers,
how I felt in mine, your grip, how you'd always come to switch
of my light, when my therapy stopped though I wanted to go,
the urge to still fill my mouth, to swallow, but nothing quenches,
how you scared me, anything, anything, I'd do anything please
to please you, what my mum said when I asked, how I suddenly I
wasn't allowed around you, my Gramparealdad hated you, I trust
him, I remember how innocently he showed me how to piss but
I remember the night where enough was enough with you, the
plots to actually kill you, none of this disturbing to me an orgasm
of confusion, frantically hiding the cum, my mess I'd made under
my pillow.

Now the world no matter how small any crowd feels stuffed in my head, won't fit like a child's lips on an adult.
I remember being on my front but slightly raised up but the worst part is

that I don't remember much.

Paul Sartre

What is a dad ?
Like a mum but male?
O' great abandoner of actual care ?
This poem doesn't concern you. I know it never would.
A listener with ears deaf of my tone?
Just an idol unknown, frozen in the practiced happy, like the
people on the back of books, in there pretend boxes of black and
white.
Surely,
Jean Paul Sartre,
Roald Dahl,
Ray Bradbury,
And Ginsberg, Walt
These are examples of dads?
Nobody taught me how to piss.
Is dad now dead? Killed by the stubbornness that he called
life, and burning constantly painful cancer, to proud to allow
themselves to die? Or the owner of a pub and the giver of a job
who didn't need to but genuinely, genuinely tried?
dad is our second word, my babel sounded like a thoughtless cry.

Are they law, abusive, fuckers of children's minds and later adult life, rising tall, remaining small, only once family by law, and never actually able to stand up with the fire of the 13 year old wronged. Fuck them then, I beat the anxiety you beat into me because I was small except for cock, you, back to your antique box. Moron.

dad
Have half
Half my skin
Half my mind
Cut my history
Have one of my eyes
Half the blood from the side that drips steady
Have half my demon. I'm a genius.
Half my semen when I build myself my child.
Have half the book I will one day write, but cut the letters vertical through the middle so they make no sense and forget themselves to rhyme.
My dad is our sex even when it's bad. My dad is my reading, my writing is my dad.
When I leave I'm my dad. My dad doesn't exist, it's not that he's missing he never was. my dad. He didn't leave, he's not even a stranger alone today, my dad. He's like a god, a writer, O' great creator of accidents. And stepdad killing fire.

I miss you. I know that impossible,
but I don't know the origin of my own face.
People outside if you do
know
please celebrate your Dad today.
Like him, you should not worry
With Walt I'll be okay
I celebrate myself.

-

The Photo Of You On A Boat.

-

When I was a child on the side of the beach with a loving
Grampa to keep the sand from my teeth I used to make paper
airplanes with my name on them "Benn" for you and the words,
"to Dad." As I hadn't yet learned to drop the cap.

Cast them off into the sea, did we, and I'd ask to use
Grampastrength to make them fly, because he was older and had
a better, paper plane throw.
He'd chuckle in that assonantal way that used an entire body, and
ironically was simply all the dad you'd need for that moment,

then the halt, the adult, he'd take my tiny hand into to his palm
and wrap it in fingers like family.

Somehow, somewhere, out there in the mixed up salt, tear taste.
I still hope.
There's still hope.
There is still hope.

Eric Blair

I don't have a simple answer. A man can not live by language
alone, this is a great shame for these letters are worth far more
than any of those numbers printed, yes, they are a measurement
but of what? I do not want money, I need money. These symbols
printed here on this page mean so, so much more, these are
the measurement of something real, these shapes measure
understanding, knowledge, even wisdom, why can't they be
that which we all we all seek so. These little odd shapes, mean
freedom, mean power, "Safety Pin revolution." or divide like
"Immigrant Vermin. " can build confidence, or dismantle us
piece by piece. The truth is we chose the numbers, we gave them
their worth, worth they didn't earn and all the while language
was teaching, language was learning. We choose the worth
of words too, we place the value, it's our choice if they mean
nothing. But, has a number moved you? Has a number made
that tremor of sound fall from you, that murmur of empathy on
the seat of your lips for someone who never truly existed? Have
you spat numbers in disgust, have your numbers ever shown
your lit up insides to the one you feel you love, is your name a
number? Your identity? Are you your pin code or your name
first? Do our numbers fill the holes left by childhood heartbreak?
Do they knit the fabric back together, and rejoin the hands of

those separate by trenches? Do our numbers dance for life in the unbound-less skies of space under our eyes? Do numbers give us anything but lost time? Can numbers rhyme? Say things that no one ever even wrote? Do numbers happen without us? We have control of numbers words will happen despite us. They are a gift we can give to others, something they can own without us loosing ownership. Language was permanent before everything. These words are my words for now, but as they flow and fill in the white they become not mine but yours, not yours but ours, we share them at the same time. Money is only ever owned by one, numbers are selfish to keep but patronizing to give. We decide the value of words, every time we write.
Words tell the truth, money lies.

I'm sorry I tried, I did try to be less poetic, more journalistic but I won't undersell my words, I decide the value, I tell the truth.

In honesty I'll keep writing for me if I can't write for you.

Why I write is simple - I don't want us to be poor.

Oslo Drip

That hole
The space gap, deep inside us
That place where we drip
In us all
Eking our insides out, filling up the earth around us all
contributing to the rise
The deepest of the human wounds

It's not an understanding we lack
But a lack of understanding
We should not seek to fill ourselves
But seek to fill ourselves.

Adam Lathbacks

you were already born
you were already form
you were already you
Not yet, were you them
Not yet were you His.
He was too late it wasn't His fault.

There you stood, bloody still and innocent,
Lead in, unknown, you were in His home
you were already thinking, already grown, already able to
contemplate, could already understand, always tried to, already
dangerous,
you were not solid wood like the all and only people He already
knew.

Why would He not take hammer to you?
Love you as only He knew
Fix all that was wrong inside
Cheerfully plain you of your top layer of skin, strip away
imperfection
He didn't know He wasn't god.

One day as he was trying, you were trying, fucking trying to be
a chair or a chest of drawers stood there in varnish while He
chipped away at the painted or tainted ends of your toes His
frustration grows, you can't stand still so

Shout.

Not around you
right into you

Shout.

An emotion as never before
hard, cold, inexorable, force, the power of adults.

Into your mouth it's forced, fleming, gagging, one day drowning,
with haired hands, holding you open, this grey anger, flesh
pushed further,
an anxiety unswallowable
you barely understand the shape of His words,

You Are Unlovable.

an almost perfect dot appears.
It's on the new outside skin in the middle of your throat,

How could you know ?

I pull that hollowing item from my stomach, it drips with the complicated
I watch your eyes taste like salt, I watch the horror in your throat
I comfort you, I feel alone. I vow that this is not your fault.

But I don't think of you. Seeing a lovers wound. What that does to you.
It was slightly too low to be my heart, but it starts.

Within the next hour it's gone away, but I feel hurt in a selfish way that a talk is needed. It would would heal but like a stupid child I poke, prod it, my fingers search for what went wrong when simply all this was was,
but a fall.

I don't think. I call myself empathetic but I can't see past my own skin.
So
Every word
Every mention
Every slip
Every notice

Every clue
Every moment
Every name
Every minute
Between kisses
Before sex
After love
Before morning
Before mourning
Any time think I should check, I feel like it's my right to know,
like I have this inherit gift of fucking control, I lift my shirt, and I
poke it, like a child misunderstanding, I show you so you can kiss
it, but I don't think.
It looks like building trust but it isn't, its building guilt there is a
difference.

It happens

I take that hollowing item form where I kept it safe, I hold it to
your throat, say
"I forgive you for all your mistakes" and "I take no blame."

I cut.

I see your nude skin,

and only because I cut you too do I notice,
that from every time in every way, with every mention of his
name, that knife we play with the knife we blame,
It hollows you too. So many damn love coloured bruises. Your
lips cracked and chapped and faded from kissing, from kissing.
From kissing my wounds.

I didn't think.
Now I do.

And still, still it is you, you who holds I still.
Fool.
Full.

Iona Unwrathe

You are mine.
I will have you all, all of you

I will take your eyes, lock them in one fixed place, allow only the
flicker. Frozen deep dark brown-black ice, with dilated fire inside.

I will take your neck, push my teeth soft and hard against it, suck
on the gap under your jaw and hum along to your badly hidden
groan.

I will take both my hands and grab you by your face, in love not
hate I will kiss your tongue hard, whilst pulling myself together I
will push you apart.

So so slow now, I will touch so lightly, so gentle, so kindly, then
grab, grasp, groan, rasp, we will breathe and I will have you.

Every contour painted dramatically in that red light, in love we
will fight.
Because You my woman, my darling, star, beloved look so fuck
damn good tonight.

You are mine.
I will have you all of you

Hands now trace you, running sparks through every vain of
you. I know when you're wet, your breathings different. You try
to retaliate but I will hold you where you should be, fucking
underneath me. All my weight is on you, I know so clearly
exactly what you want now so I do the opposite. Pull away. Pull
off my fake spotted skin and allow you to see all my within, I'm
dizzy with anticipation but I hide it so well. To you
I
look
casual.

You are mine, I will have so I slam down on you, push you, press
you, your hands try to touch me but I won't let you. Pinned by
someone with a fear of a lack of control. And I can hold.

Now my tongue is on your intricate tattoo, the painting of you,
the self portrait permanent on you.

Those bone in your hip, fuck me, oh my god it's all I want, but I
won't,

No slowly, no slowly, slowly, slowly, Iona, slow. I pull each leg

apart, I look at it, its beautiful, I've never seen one I liked before,
my tongue is on it, you shiver, you taste so damn good, I shiver,
my hands are on you my fingers in your special gap down at the
bottom of your back, we both breath in and out sharp as we come
together so soft.

its right here that all my words, my rhymes, get lost.

Iona Inceptionous

It had started the way things always do, from nothing
The light, the double light in the mirror, the me, the double I, the
sinner.
I believed in morals, I believed, in black, in white, together, apart.
As I looked in to my own apertures I recall surprise at the
glimmer as opposed to the flicker, and it was the very same I saw
within her.

The softness the caring of keys, of beauty, love despite doubt, it
carries us into each other, the piano plays on.
You, you were a mistake, the most intelligent, inspiring,
aweinspiringly incredible mistake I could ever make, and you
made me shake.

When I left the light room, saw the door reveal you, only you,
the drama of shadow pools painted on you, the glow a lack of
light seems unable to remove, I knew. But I swear when I left that
room I didn't, but I am not resolved, I wore black eyes and a black
suit. And eventually I make so   much love with you

If words could come I could sleep, all I can say is snippets,
broken, fragile, intricate more precious to me than breath,

memory of that moment within us. All I want as a writer as a man is to illustrate the way we touched.

Have I yet been inside you? I pull at the silken skins around you and playfully, comfortably we remove, those eyes, the famous muses eyes, you are the sonnet forgotten, the secret spoken. You pull my shirtskin I am broken.

It's not the eyes, it's the reveal, the conceal, the flick up, the focus the way that feels, you make me love me, that's new. I yearn to return that light to the inside of you.

You are wet, I am wet, like birth, unlike death.

Four letters three breathed syllables, not a name I primal extract, I own a.

The way your eyes rush, your back crush, the thought that we cant control this, my hands thrust, the dance the your sound, my sound, the way I was thrown, the connection the piano plays on. On

Epilogue
Building The Narrator

———

It doesn't,
he doesn't need legs to walk, or feet to stand, the feet are so
painstakingly built, added so as to put him in he context of an
Earthgravity.
He is made of clay, shaped, by human shaped hands
Faces are the hardest, noses are never quite right, mustn't let my
insecurities warp you, and it all looks inversed
again the clay eyes can't see, so it's odd to put glasses on them
but the mouth, the tongue must function
picture him,
the mouth, the tongue must function.
And the ears
I whisper him the facts. "You were abused, maybe rape, can't
remember, cheated on, maybe cheated with, your dad left,
you've never met, this is a lie, your grampas dead, this is the
truth, he who raised you, failed school, your the stupid genius,
anxiety, ADHD, depression, emitiphobia, insomnia existentialist
overly sensitive autonomic nervous system and emotional
unstable personality disorder but your not bipoler with
rapid cycle succession not even cyclothymic with rapid cycle
succession, you're the opposite of autistic but it's just as hard and
undiagnosed still, give love, cant receive, your like the sun to

You are my narrator, all my thoughts will be speach in you
You are made of clay
unreal

like me .

True

true

true

love

there's always a diminish

crawling shuddering flinching toward the flicker of language on
the lips of the hated in the eternal unmasked bleak the screen
that lights the fingers but blinds the mind the ache of existing
the disgust stickiness and sick filled skin the blood that encases
the bones chewable meat and breakable teeth the inability to
sleep and the darkness inside the true love that fuck fuck fuck
the mute ghosts with nimble fingers and the scent that lingers
the yearn the lust the lurch the full body crunch the lead the
strings the scissors in the hinges the sand that falls the flaking
the disconnection the representation of all desolation the cocks
the nothingness all is nothingness the fingers how the bend
individual yet uniquely grotesque directionless direction the
damp stabbing in the thankful dark the stumbling the somehow
ability to breath the unity the pretence of anger the lips sewn to
the lips the nails breach the palms and and force the pressing
in the hips the truth of love the inability to accept the blood all
the blood the holes the wet floods and floors from the eternal
continuing the insecurity the fact that this is more than love the
constant whittle of image the constant mute in the machinery of
the night the steady careful thoughtful destruction the dismantle

of all that was once the adults that grow up misshapen inside the claustrophobia of child suits the masks that make ugly a far more benevolent truth the words strings and strings screeds and fucking screeds everything burns the relationships a contract the signatures in thriving throbbing discos of night in jizz without permission the blood that trickles so neat down the back the men bleeding constant from there wrists the woman from their cunt the flushing of life the ejaculative or unelective orgasms of nought the unity of all in war the bodies of baby piled above the gods liquid the gurgling liquid over each other in the desperation of substance the scrambling the death by the hands the death by the lack of hands the shoulders slit the slaving the freedom the alcohol filled heathens the crown the crowd the rulers the rules the constant spin the sickening the ownership the ache of the tongue the delivery of lurch the gagging the size of the cock the size of the cock the size of my cock the gurgle the breathe under the hair the eyes turned outwards and in turn the eyes turned outwards the steps in the snow the building the building the ropes the taught the stalking the hunt submissive the control the give up the numbers the numbers etched on the shoulder in permanent raise the cum the cum the damage the only way out is of death and marriage accepted trudge of reality packed onto trains marching smaller smaller away the tangled living limbs of thorns responsibility contorted hands mixed and feet and living liquid lurching linked tendrils fixed the eyes locked the the eyes

locked the steadily approaching surrounding drop the rolls and
flaps of genitals joined still pumping pumping in the moist cold
baths the hung flesh the dangled squeezed balls the breathless
air choke and mouths filled with hair as in its collective frothing
noun or the tongue with hair as its noun the mangle of tongue
the soft parts held so wide open the vomiting cacophony yawns
all orchestral awe always always raw the booming the musk the
torture of trust the murder of lust pinned down and put to death
by the thrust or the truth unaccepted the sound to the room the
pathetic murmur of squirming the slightest squirting a squelch
like nude pasta
the cunt fucked raw the vagina penetrated by penis the willy
popped into fanny the indecent the incessant frivolous rocking
back to front that is so constantly sought over rest to fill each
others mouth with salt comes before a thought is spent to water
the human human creatures running on a chemical only housed
in the other pulling at chunks in handfuls clots of pulsing
inertia finger nails for digging at the angry tissue the search the
desperate search the found mecca the salty pool of omega and
of allah, siddhartha gautama or or pretas pure milk colourless
purity to drink from it will instantly kill me the only true
nudity the drop of nirvana frantic frantic searching the sudden
disheartening the lack of care for the shell the housing torn the
flesh sore and aching mussel the reaching
the release

the realise
The tense
The flop
The lose flaps
The instantaneously flaccid

The sudden sight readjusting the shapes of other things
remounting
The paralysis shared
Eyes fixed on plaster
Neck arched
On back
Back arced
On neck
Unaroused forever now
Slowly so slow
The necks craned first back to self
Then to face
Moving at a non pace
You have a milk moustache like a child on your
garish fixed grin
But unashame ed unguilty us
this is
true
true